When I was six, I was ready to start school. Three of my older brothers and sisters, including Walter, had already left home. Two of my brothers who still lived with us, Isaiah and John, were teenagers and worked in the fields.

I had to walk four miles to get to school. We had a different school from the white children. It was meant to be the same but our school didn't even have simple things, like paper and pencils.

I didn't let these problems stop me from becoming very good at math. I knew that if I could learn to read and do math, I could learn to do anything.

The Unforgettable
BESSIE COLEMAN

Thuo Books

I am Bessie Coleman. I was born on January 26, 1892, in Atlanta, Texas. Black families like mine worked very hard but didn't earn much money. My family moved to Waxahachie, Texas, hoping life would be better. I was only two years old at the time. I remember watching the birds flying high in the endless sky as we traveled to our new home. Little did I know that, one day, I too would fly.

Life was not easy. In 1901, my father George moved to Oklahoma as he felt life would be better there. Isaiah left for Canada and John went to Chicago.

My mother had to work even harder and longer to earn money for our family. I had to help look after my three younger sisters, even though I was only nine years old.

I now had to wait until my youngest sister was old enough to go to school before I could go back.

Even when I could go back, I couldn't go all the time. Every year at harvest time, we were not allowed to go to school. Instead, we had to help our families make money by picking cotton from summer until November or December. Picking cotton was tough but I knew I wouldn't pick cotton forever. One day, I would do great things. I had read about people doing great things in books and wanted to be like them.

When I was 23, I went to stay with my older brothers, Walter and John, and their wives in Chicago. I decided to get a job looking after people's nails at a barber shop. Life was great. I won an award for my job and had made friends in Chicago. However, things were about to change, as my brothers were sent to France to fight in the war.

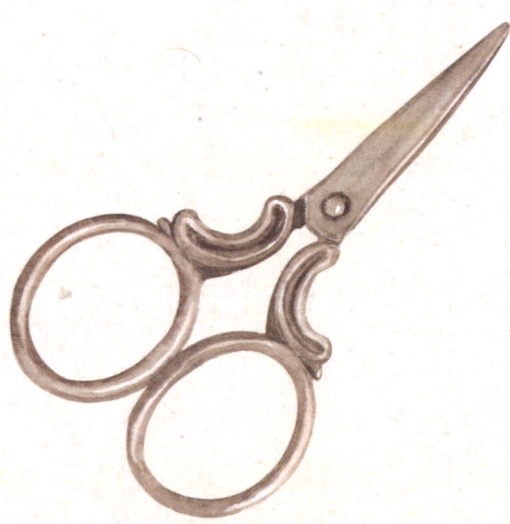

One day, after returning from the war, my brother John came into the barber shop. He laughed and told me I would never be able to fly a plane like the women he had seen in France. Suddenly, I smiled. I was going to work really hard and become a pilot.

However, no Black woman had ever been trained as a pilot and none of the American flying schools would teach me. I decided to ask Robert Abbott, who ran a newspaper called the *Chicago Defender*. He suggested that I might have better luck learning at the French flying schools. The only problem was that I could not speak French – yet!

I took French language classes and saved up money for my ticket to France. On November 20, 1920, I approached the ship I would travel on, my heart racing with excitement. Soon, I would be flying high, living my dream.

At first, even the French schools were not willing to take me. However, I finally managed to go to one of the best flying schools in France. It was hard work. I had to walk nine miles every day just to get to the airfield but nothing was going to stop me from following my dream. Soon, I earned my pilot's license, so I could fly anywhere in the world.

When I arrived back in America, everyone wanted to talk to me because I was the first Black woman to be trained as a pilot and that was big news! The next year, I went back to Europe for a while, learning how to do impressive tricks in my airplane before returning to America.

I was keen to get other people flying. I set to work saving for my own plane so I could set up a flying school. To raise money, I visited schools and communities, talking about my story and showing videos of me flying. I also did tricks at air shows in borrowed planes. Sometimes, the places where I went to fly didn't want to let Black people in. I knew this wasn't right and only flew if everyone was welcome to come and watch.

At last, I had saved up enough for a plane of my own. It was old and worn out but it was mine. I set off for the plane's first show at Palomar Park. There was a crowd of 10,000 fans waiting for me. I was so excited! Then something went terribly wrong! The plane crashed on the way to the park. I was lucky to be alive. I was unable to walk while I healed but I promised myself that, as soon as I could walk again, I would be back flying.

And fly I did. I was determined to get another plane and teach people to fly. I went back to Texas and did an air show that gave people a chance to be flown for the first time in their lives in small passenger planes. I traveled around America doing air shows until I had saved up enough money to buy another plane.

The day before doing a test flight in my new plane, I went into a restaurant and saw Robert Abbott, the man who had helped me believe in my dream. I ran over and thanked him. At the age of 34, I had already inspired a generation that they too could touch the sky and achieve great things. Now, with my new plane, I felt on top of the world.

BESSIE COLEMAN'S LEGACY

During her life, Bessie Coleman showed that anything is possible when you follow your dreams and work hard. Many women and men followed in her footsteps and learned to fly, some even going beyond the sky to the stars. Mae Jemison, the first African American woman to go into space, took Bessie Coleman's photo with her, showing that she was still inspiring people over 70 years after she became the first Black woman to earn a pilot's license.

To JJ, MM, and DC

Written and designed by Lucy Thuo
Main Illustrations by Eryanto

Copyright © Lucy Thuo, 2025
All rights reserved.

No part of this book can be reproduced in any form or by written, electronic or mechanical, including photocopying, recording, or by any information retrieval system without written permission in writing by the author.

Published by Thuo Books

Although every precaution has been taken in the preparation of this book, the publisher and author assume no responsibility for errors or omissions. Neither is any liability assumed for damages resulting from the use of information contained herein.

ISBN: 978-1-917762-17-5